STOP THE STONE MONSTERS!

Written by Helen Murray

Penguin
Random
House

Senior Editor Helen Murray
Editor Rosie Peet
Project Art Editor Jon Hall
Pre-production Producer Kavita Varma
Senior Producer Lloyd Robertson
Managing Editor Paula Regan
Design Manager Jo Connor
Art Director Lisa Lanzarini
Publisher Julie Ferris
Publishing Director Simon Beecroft

First published in Great Britain in 2017 by
Dorling Kindersley Limited
80 Strand, London WC2R 0RL
A Penguin Random House Company

10 9 8 7 6 5 4 3 2 1
001–298008–Mar/2017
Page design copyright © 2017 Dorling Kindersley Limited

A CIP catalogue record for this book
is available from the British Library.

ISBN: 978-0-24128-024-9

Printed and bound in China

www.LEGO.com
www.dk.com

A WORLD OF IDEAS:
SEE ALL THERE IS TO KNOW

Contents

A Time of Peace

The land of Knighton is at peace.
The five hero knights enjoy
some quiet time.
But a dark cloud is looming
over the land...

Macy

Lance

Aaron

Clay

Axl

The Cloud of Monstrox

The dark cloud is the evil
Cloud of Monstrox.
It blasts stones with lightning.
The blasts turn the stone objects
into scary monsters!

The Cloud of
Monstrox

Stone
Monster

An Evil Plan

The Cloud plans to turn the
whole of Knighton to dust.
The Cloud blasts Jestro the jester.
This makes Jestro bad!
Now the evil Cloud has
an evil helper.

STONE MONSTERS

The Cloud creates a huge army of stone soldiers. Meet some of the scary Stone Monsters.

Gargoyle

Reex and Roog

Ruina

Rogul

Grimroc

Brickster

Heroes to the Rescue?

Will the five knights be able to defeat the Cloud, Jestro and the Stone Monsters? Jestro's new battle vehicle looks terrifying!

Awesome Vehicles

The knights are ready
to save Knighton!
Clay takes to the skies in
his Falcon Fighter Blaster.
Aaron knocks down monsters
on his Rock Climber bike.

Merlok 2.0

Combo NEXO Powers

The monsters are very strong. Luckily, the knights have a digital wizard friend, Merlok 2.0.

Merlok 2.0 sends the knights three powers at once. Three powers combined can beat the Stone Monsters!

From: Robin
To: NEXO KNIGHTS™ team

Subject: **Battle Suits**

Dear friends,

I have good news!

Your Battle Suits are ready.
These awesome suits can
upload three powers together.
They will help you to beat
the Stone Monsters.

Robin

Clay

Macy

Lance

Aaron

Axl

Ultimate Battle

The knights wear their
new Battle Suits to fight
the Stone Monsters.

The combined powers turn
the Stone Monsters to dust.
Knighton is saved.
Hooray!

Quiz

1. What is the name of this dark cloud?

2. What does the cloud turn stone objects into?

3. Who is this?

4. Who flies the Falcon Fighter Blaster?

5. How many powers combined can beat the Stone Monsters?

Index

A Note to Parents

THIS BOOK is part of an exciting four-level reading series for children, developing the habit of reading widely for both pleasure and information.

Beautiful illustrations and superb full-colour images combine with engaging, easy-to-read narratives to offer a fresh approach to each subject in the series. Each book is guaranteed to capture a child's interest while developing his or her reading skills, general knowledge and love of reading.

The four levels of reading books are aimed at different reading abilities, enabling you to choose the books that are exactly right for your child:

Level 1: Learning to read
Level 2: Beginning to read
Level 3: Beginning to read alone
Level 4: Reading alone

The "normal" age at which a child begins to read can be anywhere from three to eight years old. Adult participation through the lower levels is very helpful for providing encouragement, discussing storylines and sounding out unfamiliar words.

No matter which level you select, you can be sure that you are helping your child learn to read, then read to learn!